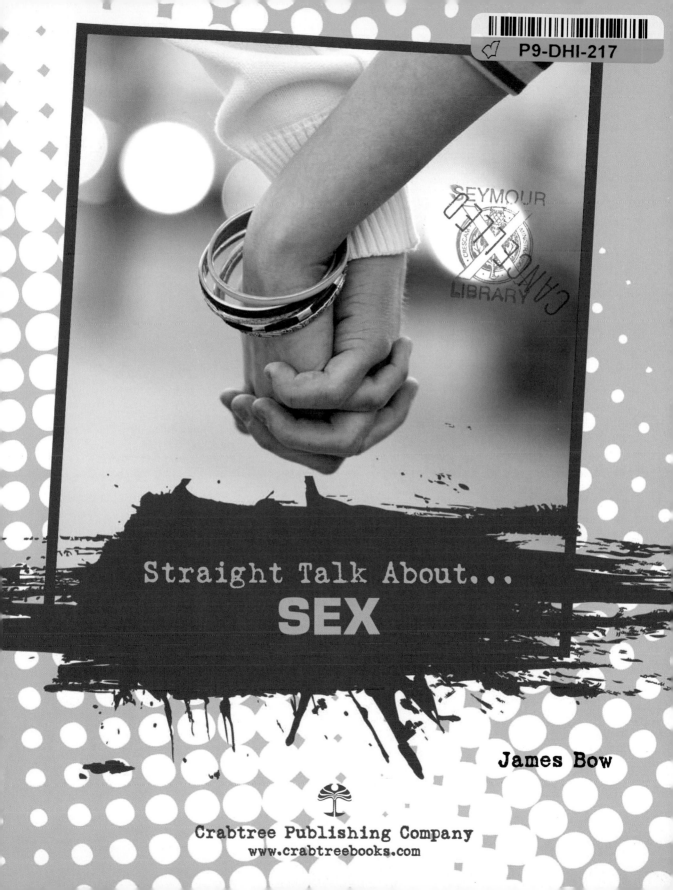

Straight Talk About...
SEX

James Bow

Crabtree Publishing Company
www.crabtreebooks.com

Straight Talk About...

Developed and produced by: Netscribes Inc.

Author: James Bow

Publishing plan research and development:
Sean Charlebois, Reagan Miller
Crabtree Publishing Company

Project Controller: Sandeep Kumar G

Editorial director: Kathy Middleton

Editors: John Perritano, Molly Aloian

Proofreader: Kathy Middleton

Art director: Dibakar Acharjee

Designer: Shruti Aggarwal

Cover design: Margaret Amy Salter

**Production coordinator and
prepress technician:** Margaret Amy Salter

Print coordinators: Katherine Berti,
Margaret Amy Salter

Consultant: Carla Lundblade, M.S., L.P.C., N.C.C.

Photographs:
Cover: iStockphoto/Thinkstock; Title page: dean bertoncelj/Shutterstock Inc.; p.4:Alexander Raths/Shutterstock Inc.; p.6:Yen Hung/Shutterstock Inc.; p.8:Sebastian Kaulitzki/Shutterstock Inc.; p.9:Monkey Business Images/Shutterstock Inc.; p.10:Joyce Vincent/Shutterstock Inc.; p.12:vita khorzhevska/Shutterstock Inc.; p.13:WilleeCole/Shutterstock Inc.; p.14:Stanislav Popov/Shutterstock Inc.; p.16:Fedorov Oleksiy/Shutterstock Inc.; p.18:vadim kozlovsky/Shutterstock Inc.; p.20:MitarArt/Shutterstock Inc.; p.22:Africa Studio/Shutterstock Inc.; p.25:O2creationz/Shutterstock Inc.; p.26:Kamira/Shutterstock Inc.; p.28:bikeriderlondon/Shutterstock Inc.; p.30:bogdan ionescu/Shutterstock Inc.; p.32:Marilyn Nieves/Istockphoto.com; p.33:Yuri Arcurs/Shutterstock Inc.; p.34:Iakov Filimonov/Shutterstock Inc.; p.35:Kieren Welch/Shutterstock Inc.; p.36:Monkey Business Images/Shutterstock Inc.; p.39:Monkey Business Images/Shutterstock Inc.; p.40:Pressmaster/Shutterstock Inc.; p.41:Monkey Business Images/Shutterstock Inc.; p.42:suzanna/Shutterstock Inc.

SEYMOUR LIBRARY

Library and Archives Canada Cataloguing in Publication

Bow, James, 1972-
    Sex / James Bow.

(Straight talk about--)
Includes index.
Issued also in electronic format.
ISBN 978-0-7787-2186-4 (bound).--ISBN 978-0-7787-2193-2 (pbk.)

    1. Sex instruction for children. I. Title. II. Series: Straight talk about-- (St. Catharines, Ont.)

HQ53.B68 2013   j649'.65   C2013-901021-1

Library of Congress Cataloging-in-Publication Data

Bow, James.
  Sex / James Bow.
       pages cm. -- (Straight talk about...)
  Includes index.
  Audience: Grade 4 to 6.
  ISBN 978-0-7787-2186-4 (reinforced library binding) -- ISBN 978-0-7787-2193-2 (pbk.) -- ISBN 978-1-4271-9069-7 (electronic pdf) -- ISBN 978-1-4271-9123-6 (electronic html)
 1. Sex instruction for children--Juvenile literature. I. Title.

HQ53.B69 2013
613.9071--dc23
                                          2013004909

Crabtree Publishing Company

www.crabtreebooks.com   1-800-387-7650

Printed in the USA/052013/JA20130412

Published in Canada
Crabtree Publishing
616 Welland Ave.
St. Catharines, ON
L2M 5V6

Published in the United States
Crabtree Publishing
PMB 59051
350 Fifth Avenue, 59th Floor
New York, New York 10118

Published in the United Kingdom
Crabtree Publishing
Maritime House
Basin Road North, Hove
BN41 1WR

Published in Australia
Crabtree Publishing
3 Charles Street
Coburg North
VIC, 3058

CONTENTS

Ben sits on the chair in the doctor's office. He is sick. He doesn't feel sick, but for the past week he's felt a burning sensation when he urinates. Ben told the doctor about the problem. She ordered some tests. The tests came back positive for gonorrhea. Ben has heard of gonorrhea. It's a sexually transmitted disease, or STD. He learned in school that if the disease goes untreated, he could become very ill.

Ben tried to figure out how he got the illness. He and his girlfriend, Jennifer, have not had intercourse. They did, however, have oral sex. But before he started dating Jennifer, he had had oral sex with Erica, too. He never told Jennifer. Did he get the disease from Erica? Ben worries that he may have given Jennifer gonorrhea, too. But what if Ben got it from Jennifer? Does that mean she cheated?

The doctor told Ben that a person can in fact get an STD from oral sex. Ben now has to tell Jennifer about his STD. He has to tell Erica, too. They both might have the disease.

Introduction
Risky Behavior

Ben, Jennifer, and Erica aren't alone. Each year, 570,000 teenagers become infected with gonorrhea. Additionally, more teens are infected with other STDs, including HIV, chlamydia, herpes, and the human papillomavirus (HPV). Some teens don't even know they're infected until serious health problems occur later on.

Getting an STD is a very real possibility for teens who are sexually active. So are unplanned pregnancies, which affect about 750,000 teens every year. Most teens either don't know the risks involved in having unprotected sex or don't believe it will happen to them. Too many find out the hard way.

"I first saw Tanya in English class. She was hot. One day I got up enough courage and asked her to go on a date. I was surprised when she said 'yes.' Soon, we were hooking up. At first, we'd just kiss. Then we began to play with each other. It was fun. Now we're talking about doing more." Tom, aged 16.

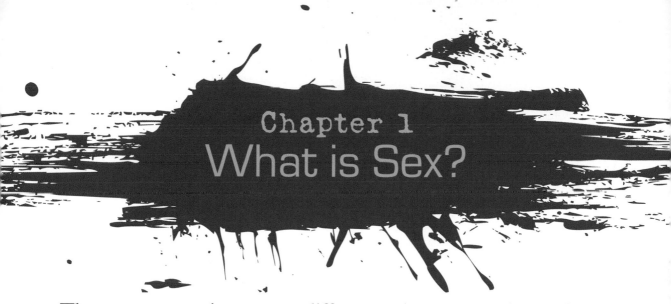

Chapter 1
What is Sex?

There are many important differences between males and females, especially when it comes to their bodies. Each has different **genitalia**, or sex organs. A male has a **penis** and a **scrotum**. A female has a **vagina**. Sex organs allow humans to **reproduce**, or make babies. Each person is born with genitalia, but a female cannot have children until she reaches **puberty**.

Once puberty begins, things start to change. The body releases hormones, which change the shape of the body. Hormones are chemicals your body produces. They help you to grow into an adult. Puberty often starts at age 12, but it can begin as young as 9, or as late as 17.

The Change Begins

During puberty, hair begins growing on **pubic** areas and under the arms. Males grow hair on their face. Their voice begins to change. Females develop breasts, and their hips become wider. They also begin **menstruation**. Boys are turning into men, and girls are turning into women.

How Sex Works

To make babies, males and females must have sex. During sex, a male's erect penis enters a female's vagina. The male **ejaculates** in the vagina, releasing millions of **sperm**. The sperm travels into the female's **uterus** and through her **fallopian tubes**, where it meets an egg released by one of the female's **ovaries**.

The egg is **fertilized** when the sperm and egg meet. The egg then travels down the fallopian tube, into the uterus, and attaches to its wall. Inside the uterus, the egg, which is now an **embryo**, develops into a **fetus**. Approximately nine months later, a baby is born.

Not Just About Babies

If sex were about only making babies, we would have sex as animals do— by instinct, only at certain times of the year. Sex is something we choose to do. Sex is a way for two people to express their feelings of attraction and love for each other.

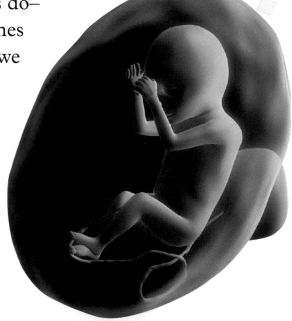

A woman's body provides the fetus with everything it needs to survive.

First Time

It's natural for preteens and teenagers to be curious about sex. The decision whether or not to have sex relies greatly on a person's sense of responsibility, to themselves, as well as to a potential partner. Governments help make us aware of this by creating "age of consent" laws. These laws set the age at which people are legally considered old enough to decide on their own whether or not to have sex. In many places that age is 16, but in some places it's as high as 18.

This age range reflects the average age that teenagers in the United States and Canada have sex for the first time. It is important to remember that this is only an average and will not be everybody's experience .

It's natural for teens to feel attraction to each other, but sex is only one way to show you care for another person.

"You should only have sex when you're ready, because it's overrated." Anonymous girl, aged 17.

Chapter 2
Sex and Sexuality

Sexuality is different from sex. Your sex–or gender– is defined by what sexual organs you are born with. Your sexuality, however, is more than that. Your sexuality is whether you're attracted to males, females, both, or none of the above.

Sex between males and females is called heterosexual sex. However, heterosexual sex isn't the only way humans can feel sexual attraction. Some males are attracted to other males. Some females are attracted to other females. Same-sex attraction is called homosexuality. Some people are bisexual, or attracted to both sexes. Some people may be transgendered, which means they see themselves as being a different sex than the sex organs they were born with. For example, a boy may have male genitalia and wear boys' clothing, but he may feel like a girl, want to be a girl, and sees himself as a girl.

Private Lives

If you're attracted to a member of the same sex, and that person feels the same way, and you decide to have a loving relationship together, that is no one's business but your own. The law agrees. In fact, even marriage laws in many states and in Canada are changing to include same-sex couples.

It is important to remember that we are all different. You shouldn't have to change who you are to fit what other people think you should be. You should make your own informed choices.

Sex is Still Sex

When it comes to being sexually active, homosexual and bisexual couples face the same potential risks as heterosexual couples. The chance of contracting STDs remains the same. The laws of consent still apply.

Regardless of whom you are attracted to, your first sexual experience should be with somebody you trust.

Same-sex couples are becoming increasingly accepted in society.

Asexuality

There are people who feel no sexual attraction to any member of either sex. They are asexual. While it might seem that people who have no interest in sex might find life less complicated, that's not always true.

An asexual person might listen as a friend talks about how attractive some person is, or how hot a celebrity looks. An asexual person does not experience the same excitement. This can make an asexual person wonder if something is wrong with him or her. He or she might even decide to try sex in order to just fit in. That is not a good reason to have sex.

An asexual person does not see sex as a major part of a relationship.

If you feel no attraction to either boys or girls, don't worry. There's nothing wrong with you. In fact, there are other people who feel the same way you do.

"My first crush was in sixth grade on a girl named Erica. At the time, and for many years to come, I thought nothing of it. Now, I identify as lesbian... I only admitted all of this to myself a few months ago." Kirsten, aged 18.

Chapter 3
Risky Business

Having sex is a big decision with consequences that can change your life. You need to be aware of the risks, which might include an unplanned pregnancy or contracting a sexually transmitted disease.

Heterosexual sex can result in a pregnancy. Sometimes, the pregnancy is exactly what a couple was hoping to achieve. Unfortunately, most teens don't fall into that category. What if you became pregnant? Having a child is a big responsibility and a lot of hard work.

Anyone who is sexually active, whether they are heterosexual, bisexual, or homosexual, can be at risk of contracting a sexually transmitted disease. Most STDs are infections caused by bacteria, parasites, or **viruses**. STDs spread when people engage in any sexual activity—not just intercourse. Anyone who is sexually active must protect themselves against STDs.

AIDs—A Devastating Disease

AIDS (acquired immune deficiency syndrome) is a deadly STD. People develop AIDS after being infected with HIV (human immunodeficiency virus). HIV is passed by blood-to-blood contact, and the sharing of body fluids.

Once in your body, HIV attacks your **immune system**, targeting and killing white blood cells. Without white blood cells, your body can't fight off common infections. HIV doesn't kill you, but it makes it easier for all sorts of other viruses and bacteria to kill you.

When HIV first appeared in the 1970s and the 1980s, most people infected were gay, or homosexual, men. As a result, many people believed at first that HIV affects mostly homosexuals. This is a myth. Any type of unprotected sex, whether between homosexuals or heterosexuals, can pass on HIV.

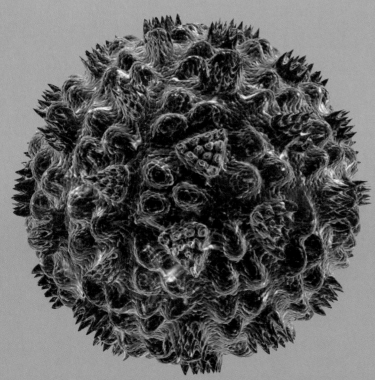

This is an enlarged photo of the virus that causes AIDS.

Types of STDs

There are many different STDs. Some can be cured and some cannot.

Genital human papillomavirus (HPV) is the most common STD. Many people have the virus and don't know it. It can be spread through kissing or touching. Symptoms include warts around the penis, vagina, or throat. Condoms and **dental dams** help reduce the risk of spreading HPV, but they have to be used correctly every time you have sex. There are also **vaccines** that can prevent HPV.

The Centers for Disease Control recommends that boys and girls aged 11 and 12 be vaccinated against HPV.

Other STDs

Syphilis, gonorrhea, and herpes are all STDs. Decades ago, people didn't know much about STDs. Today, there is a lot of information about each of these diseases. You can get good information from your doctor, at the library, or from reading credible Web sites on the Internet. At the end of this book are several informative Web sites that can help.

Important Questions About STDs

Q: How do I get an STD?
A: STDs are often spread when two partners have unprotected sex, but this is not the only way. You can get an STD through intimate touching, such as kissing or touching your partner's genitals.

Q: How can I tell if my partner has an STD?
A: Many STDs don't have symptoms that we recognize. So, you can't easily see if someone has an STD. The only way to know for sure is if you and your partner are tested by a doctor. You might have an STD and not know it, and then pass it on to your partner.

Q: How do I prevent STDs?
A: There are some ways to protect yourself from STDs. Keep reading to find out how. There are also people you can call and information on the Internet.

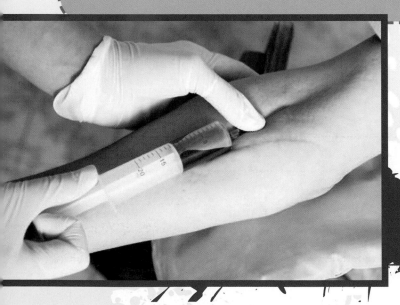

A blood test is an easy way to tell if you have an STD.

Myths About Sex

There are many myths about sex. These myths often cause people to make bad choices.

MYTH: You can't get pregnant the first time you have sex. Or, you can't get an STD if you only have sex once.

FACT: There is no difference between the first time you have sex and the hundredth time. You only need to have sex once to become pregnant or get an STD.

MYTH: You can't get pregnant if you have sex standing up. Or, you can't get pregnant if you jump around a lot after sex.

FACT: It doesn't matter what sexual position you use, or what you do afterward. Once sperm goes into a woman's vagina, it's not coming out, even if she takes a hot bath.

MYTH: If you have sex in a pool or a hot tub, the chlorine and heat will kill any STDs you might catch.

FACT: No. The vagina is a good place to protect both sperm and an STD. You can get pregnant if you have sex in a hot tub, and you can get STDs as well.

MYTH: Masturbation is unhealthy.

FACT: No, it's not. Masturbation is when you touch your own sexual parts to feel pleasure. It's perfectly healthy. Masturbation is a good way to make your body feel sexual pleasure without the risks of getting pregnant or an STD.

"I had sex with someone I shouldn't have. When I was tested [for an STD]... it was scary. The wait was awful. I'm just thankful that I was ok. If he is too stupid to use a condom, he doesn't deserve to have sex with you." Tanya, aged 16.

Chapter 4
Protecting Yourself

You can reduce your chances of getting pregnant and getting STDs by using birth control and practicing safe sex. You can buy birth control devices at your local drug store or from a doctor. There are also many ways to practice safe sex and prevent STDs.

The birth control pill is the most popular **contraceptive**. You may have heard your mother, or an aunt, or older sister talk about "the pill," as it is commonly known. Its official name is the combined oral contraception pill. The pill uses hormones, such as estrogen and progestogen, to trick a woman's body into believing it's pregnant. As a result, the pill stops the ovaries from releasing eggs. If an egg isn't released, a pregnancy can't take place.

Many women in the United States started taking the pill in the 1960s. It allowed them to have more control over their bodies and not have to worry about getting pregnant every time they had sex.

The Risks

The pill, however, does have risks, including the potential for dangerous blood clots and depression. Only a very small percentage of users, however, are affected by these and other side effects. Doctors generally agree there are more risks during pregnancy and childbirth than there are from taking the pill.

The pill must be taken every day for it to work effectively. Forget a dose and you could get pregnant. It is also important to remember that the pill does not prevent sexually transmitted diseases.

Condoms

A condom is another common contraceptive. A condom slips tightly over the male's erect penis. When he ejaculates during sex, the condom stops sperm from entering the female's vagina. The condom also prevents STDs. Condoms are often coated with spermicide, a special substance that kills sperm and STDs. Spermicides help make condoms extra effective in case they tear.

More than 5 billion condoms are sold around the world each year.

Risks of the Condom

Condoms are not risk-free, however. Condoms are made of a thin, strong material called latex. Some people are allergic to latex. People who are allergic to latex can use polyurethane condoms. Polyurethane is a type of plastic.

Condoms can sometimes break. They might also be difficult to put on quickly. Condoms come with instructions. Read them beforehand so you know how to put one on properly. If you touch a condom to the tip of your penis and discover it is inside out, throw the condom away and put a new one on. If you put a condom on incorrectly, some sperm can make it inside a woman's vagina. That makes it possible for a woman to get pregnant and for an STD to spread.

For a condom to work, it must be put on properly every time before the penis comes into contact with the vagina. A penis can leak sperm before ejaculation, and even just touching an erect, unprotected penis against a vagina can be enough to pass on an STD or cause a pregnancy.

By the Numbers

Two condoms are not better than one. If a condom breaks, you might be tempted to use two at once for extra protection. Don't. The condoms can rub against each other, causing friction, making them even more likely to tear.

The Intrauterine Device (IUD)

Another form of contraception is called the Intrauterine Device (IUD), a T-shaped object inserted into a woman's uterus. Early IUDs worked by irritating the wall of the uterus, preventing the egg from attaching. Today's IUDs are coated with hormones. That means they work just like the pill.

An IUD can work for up to five years without having to be replaced. Like the pill, IUDs do not prevent the spread of STDs.

What Doesn't Work

Several methods of contraception don't prevent pregnancies or stop the spread of STDs. For example, the withdrawal method is unreliable. The withdrawal method is when the man pulls his unprotected penis from his partner's vagina before ejaculating. However, some sperm can leak out of the penis while sex is taking place.

Out of Rhythm

The rhythm method requires partners to have sex only during certain times during the woman's menstrual cycle. In theory, a woman is only fertile for a few days after her ovaries release an egg into her fallopian tubes. Sex outside of that time does not result in pregnancy.

However, sperm can live for a long time inside a woman's body. It's very difficult to predict when her body will release an egg. There's no time during a woman's menstrual cycle when pregnancy is 100 percent impossible.

Oral Sex is Still Sex

Oral sex is not necessarily safe sex. Receiving and giving oral sex can transmit STDs. Sexually transmitted diseases are mostly viruses or bacteria that enter the body during sex through tiny cuts in the skin or mucus membranes. Any form of sexual contact creates a chance of transmission. Herpes, gonorrhea, syphilis, hepatitis A, B, and C, and HIV all can be transmitted through oral sex.

Condoms and dental dams can help reduce the risk of getting an STD from oral sex.

Condoms and dental dams can prevent an STD, such as syphilis, pictured here in this magnified photo.

By the Numbers

The National Center for Health Statistics asked 2,800 sexually active American teens what birth control they used. Ninety-five percent said they had used a condom at least once; 58 percent said they used the withdrawal method; 17 percent said they used the rhythm method.

Source: National Center for Health Statistics

"I trusted him. I trusted that he would not have sex with anyone else. Now, I have an STD. What am I going to do?" Carolina, aged 15.

Chapter 5
Trust

Trust is central to any sexual relationship. Before engaging in sex, individuals have to determine whether or not they trust their partner. Do they trust that their partner does not have an STD? Can they trust their partner when they say they have taken precautions to limit the risk of pregnancy and STDs?

Before engaging in sex, you and your partner should be tested for STDs. Remember, it's possible to have an STD and not know it. You should always use a condom even if you are using birth control pills.

When two people trust, love, and respect one another, they must also act responsibly toward each other. Only then can sex can be a wonderful and healthy part of a relationship.

Waiting for Sex

As you now know, the decision to become sexually active comes with risks. There is no 100-percent-effective method of birth control. Condoms have only a 95 to 98 percent success rate in stopping pregnancies. Condoms can break, or they can be put on improperly. The same problems that prevent a condom from stopping pregnancies also allow STDs to be passed between partners. Even with condoms, sex carries risks.

If you aren't ready to deal with sex and all its possible consequences, then it is best not to have sex at all. This is a practice called abstinence. Although it might sound like everybody at your school is having sex, the reality is that most teenagers don't. Fifty-four percent of teenagers have not had sex by the age of 19.

Despite what your friends might be telling you, most teenagers do not have sex until they are much older.

Does Abstinence Work?

The idea of teenagers having sex makes many parents uncomfortable. Some parents have asked educators to teach abstinence as the only method of birth control.

In theory, abstinence is a surefire way to avoid pregnancy and STDs. However, in communities where only abstinence is taught, the number of teenage pregnancies and cases of STDs generally increases, not decreases.

Experts say teenagers who are taught abstinence as the only method of birth control are put at a disadvantage. Feelings can become very intense when a couple is in physical contact. Their resistance can easily weaken. Because they don't know any other way to limit the risks of pregnancy or STDs when engaging in sexual activity, they are more likely to have unprotected sex.

By the Numbers

In 2008, researchers found that states such as Connecticut, Massachusetts, New Hampshire, and Vermont, which taught all forms of birth control, had a birth rate of 25 out of 1,000 teens aged 15 to 19. States that taught abstinence only, like Mississippi, Oklahoma, and Texas, had a birth rate of 60 pregnancies per 1,000 teens.

Source: National Center for Health Statistics

"There are virgins around. It's not like they are an extinct species." Shauda, aged 19.

Chapter 6
Social Attitudes

You might one day feel a lot of pressure to have sex. Your partner might be pushing you. You may feel as though everyone around you is having sex. Your parents might have strict ideas about when you can have sex.

To make things worse, sex seems to be all around you. Advertisers try to make certain products look sexy so they can sell more goods. Models in magazines and on television wear revealing clothes and strike sexy poses.

The media is fascinated with sex, often reporting about celebrity divorces and sexual **exploits**. There's sex on TV. There's sex in the movies. Sometimes the messages you see and hear are conflicting. Often, people make sex seem dirty and wrong. Sex seems to be something that everyone wants but isn't allowed to have. How do you deal with these inconsistent messages and make your own decisions?

Peer Pressure

No doubt you hear a lot about sex from friends and schoolmates. Boys and girls both joke about sex. Some even brag about having sex. Others might admire a boy or girl who claims to have had sex with many partners. Boys and girls that have no interest in having sex are teased with suggestions that they are gay or lesbian.

Sometimes girls and boys harshly judge those who do not want to date. They make fun of them. They call them names. Teens will also pressure their friends to have sex. According to one survey by the Kaiser Family Foundation, one out of three boys, ages 15 to 17, said they felt pressure to have sex, generally from male friends. Twenty three percent of girls said they felt the same pressure by their friends.

When it comes to sex, peer pressure can be overwhelming.

Sexting

The Internet has added a new dimension to sexual attitudes and behaviors. Many teenagers have cell phones with cameras. Many teenagers have snapped pictures of themselves while half-dressed or undressed, or in sexy poses. They've sent these pictures to friends for a laugh. They've sent them to people they're attracted to as a way of flirting. This is called sexting.

Sexting might seem harmless at first, but it is not. It is easy for others to make copies of these pictures or videos and post them online or text them to friends.

New stories are on the rise of boys and girls whose private images have been broadcast to their schools, friends, and families. Harassed by their schoolmates and made to feel ashamed, some have even committed suicide.

Never send suggestive photos of yourself to anyone, not even someone you trust. If you are tempted to send such photos to a boyfriend or a girlfriend, remind yourself that trust can easily be betrayed.

Sending sexy pictures to a boy or a girl can often lead to bullying and embarrassment.

Parent Trap

You might feel that you can't talk to your parents or guardians about sex. You're afraid they will be shocked or angry that you're even thinking about having sex. Still, try to communicate with them.

Parents have a wealth of experience regarding sex and relationships. It might prove beneficial to talk with them if you are having a problem.

Your parents might be uncomfortable—they see the same conflicting messages you do. They remember their own first times and are worried about what you are going through.

If you get up the courage to open up to your parents, they will more than likely answer your questions. They'll tell you what they feel is the right thing to do. It may be different from what you want to do, but that's only because your parents might have different attitudes towards sex and want you to be safe.

It's About You

At the end of the day, you should be the one who makes the choices that affect your life. Get all the facts, check them twice, and make your own decisions. It's hard to ignore bad peer pressure. It takes courage to stand up to bullies. It is much better to be yourself and do what is right for you.

Sex is something that you should decide for yourself to do. When you decide you are responsible enough to have sex, it should be with someone you love, trust, and respect, and who loves, trusts, and respects you. The people who love you and want you to succeed will have good advice for you, but the final choice is yours to make.

You don't have to live up to the media's messages or cave into peer pressure. Don't let anyone force you to do something you don't want to do. Find the people who will help you make good decisions.

You control your body, no one else does. At the end of the day, the decisions you make are your own.

"Sex is not what you expect! Not for me anyways. It didn't hurt, but it didn't feel good either. Honestly, sex is overrated. For me, having sex didn't thrill me. And if you are considering sex, make sure your first time is with someone who you really love." Tammy, aged 17.

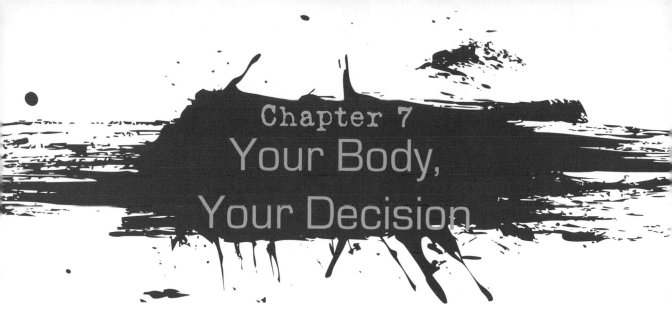

Chapter 7
Your Body, Your Decision

For some, sex is about control. Nobody should force you to do anything you don't want to do. Nobody should trick you. This is your body. This is your choice.

A young person's first sexual experience may happen because of pressure from a partner. In a 2003 study in the United States, 89 percent of girls reported feeling pressured by boys to have sex, while 49 percent of boys reported feeling the same pressure from girls.

Pressure to have sex comes in many forms including asking repeatedly, begging, and threats. If you feel pressure to have sex, remember that no one who loves and respects you would want to put you into an uncomfortable situation.

Harassment

A person pressuring you for sex may yell at you, insult you, or threaten to injure you. It happens to both boys and girls. These are criminal acts called sexual harassment.

Nobody has the right to bully you into having sex. No one has the right to make you feel uncomfortable if you choose not to have sex. In these situations, you need to leave, get help, and perhaps call the police.

Sexual harassment also includes comments that make you uncomfortable. This can include inappropriate jokes, conversations, whistling, pictures, or comments.

If these things make you uncomfortable, you have the right to ask these people to stop. If they don't stop, get help, or tell someone in charge, such as a teacher, principal, or community resource officer.

Sexual Assault and Rape

Sexual assault and rape are violent crimes. A sexual assault occurs when a person forces or threatens another person to perform a sexual act that he or she does not want to do.

Both women and men can be raped and both can be rapists. Rape is not about sex, love, or passion. It is a horrible violation. You have a right to fight back and get help.

Date Rape

Date rape is forced sex that occurs between two people who know each other. They can be family members or friends. The rapist might not be dating the victim. Because the victim knows the rapist, he or she trusts that person, which makes it easier for the rape to take place.

Alcohol is often involved in date rape. Date rapists often put drugs in a drink. These drugs often make the victim unaware of what's happening. Victims describe feeling paralyzed and having blurred vision. They often don't remember the crime. Victims sometimes don't realize they've been raped until there are medical problems, including STDs or pregnancy.

Date rape often involves spiking drinks with drugs.

Drugged

Date rape drugs are sometimes used in bars, or at large parties where you may not know or trust all the people. To avoid becoming a victim, go to parties with a friend, and be clear with your friend and your parents about where you'll be, when you'll be leaving, and when you will get home. Have your friends around you so they can help you if you need it, and always be around to help your friends.

Under the Influence

If you're feeling pressure to have sex, adding alcohol to the mix can be dangerous. Alcohol affects a person's control of impulsive behavior. This makes it harder for people to make good decisions. It might lead you to have sex when you otherwise would not have wanted to.

When deciding whether or not to engage in sexual activity, you definitely need a clear head and all your wits about you.

Making sure your friends are around is a good idea when going to parties.

Getting Help

If you have been sexually assaulted you need to call a rape crisis center. It can be found in the phone book. Counselors will help you call the police and get you to a hospital or a clinic.

Here are three things you should know about rape:

- Rape is never your fault.
- You need to seek medical help.
- You should get help to deal with your feelings.

Nurses and doctors specializing in rape cases will examine you and collect evidence that can help put the rapist in jail. They will also see if you need emergency birth control. Rape crisis counselors can help get you through this scary process and get you on the road to recovery.

If you have been sexually assaulted, get help. Rape crisis centers have counselors ready to help you deal with the crime.

By the Numbers

A survey by the National Campaign to Prevent Teen Pregnancy found that 7 percent of youth used alcohol the first time they had sex, while 6 percent used alcohol the most recent time they had sex.

Source: National Campaign to Prevent Teen Pregnancy

41

"I was 14 when I started having sex. I became pregnant at 15 and had my son at 16. I was in no way prepared for a pregnancy or raising a baby... I wish I had waited until I was older." Annabeth, aged 17.

Chapter 8
You Are Not Alone

It will be easier for you to make decisions about sex if you ask questions and talk openly and honestly with people you trust.

It's okay to talk to your parents. They have experienced the same worries you are experiencing.

Sharing your worries with a friend is helpful because everyone has the same questions about sex. Friends protect each other and are often the first people a person turns to for advice. Talk to your boyfriend or girlfriend. What does he or she want out of the relationship? What do you want?

If you feel there is no one you can turn to for help, pick up the phone. There are centers where kids can talk about their problems. They will answer your questions, offer you support, and connect you with people who can help you.

You'll never forget your first time, and hopefully not regret it, either. The important thing is sex is an experience that two people should enjoy together in a loving, thoughtful, and respectful way.

Hot Topics
Q&A

Am I the only virgin at my school? Everybody is talking about sex. Sometimes it seems that everybody is having it except me.

A: Don't believe everything you hear. Around 56 percent of people don't have sex until after they graduate high school. That doesn't stop some people who haven't had sex yet from talking about it or bragging.

Will the first person I have sex with be the person I marry?

A: Waiting until marriage to have sex is totally up to you. However, if you fall madly in love with someone, and want to marry them just so you can have sex, be careful. You are young and will likely have crushes, and even loving relationships with more than one person before you get married. You need to be just as sure about marriage as you are about being ready to have sex.

Can condoms be reused?

A: No. Don't even try.

I've just started taking the birth control pill. Is it safe to have sex without a condom?

A: It takes time for the pill's hormones to build up in your body. It can take up to a month before you can be sure the pill is working. Remember, the pill doesn't protect against STDs, a condom does.

What is an orgasm?

A: An orgasm is one way your body reacts to sex. During sex, partners touch and feel parts of one another's bodies, sending messages to the brain. It feels good. Your body physically responds to these sensations and feelings gradually, until they are released in a big rush. Your blood pressure rises. Your breathing becomes deeper. Your face becomes flushed. Suddenly, you'll have an orgasm.

For boys, an orgasm usually happens when they ejaculate. For girls, an incredible amount of nerve and muscle tension builds up, until their bodies involuntarily release it all at once. Not every sexual act ends in an orgasm.

How do I know when I'm ready to have sex?

A: Only you can answer that question. Do you have a partner that you love, respect, and trust? Does your partner love, trust, and respect, you? Do you feel comfortable about the idea of having sex? Are you feeling pressured into having sex? Have you and your partner talked about having sex? Have you thought about the risks? What will this do to your relationship?

Before having sex, you and your partner should both be tested for STDs. You should agree to engage in safe sex, using a condom.

Other Resources

There are a number of organizations and Web sites out there to help people who have questions about sex or sexuality. If you want to know more, or if you need help, give these places a call, or look them up on the Internet.

In the United States

Planned Parenthood

1-800-230-PLAN

www.plannedparenthood.org

Planned Parenthood provides many services, including birth control, pregnancy tests, tests for STDs including HIV, breast exams, and abortions. They also offer advice to men, women, and teens about pregnancy and sexual health. The 24-hour hotline will direct you to the clinic nearest to you.

National Sexual Assault Hotline

1-800-656-HOPE

www.rainn.org

If you have been sexually assaulted or raped, counselors will respond to provide advice and help, and point you to the nearest rape crisis center.

Teen Line
1-800-852-8336

www.teenlineonline.org

A teen help line and Web site based in California, run by teens for teens, offering counseling and advice.

StayTeen.org
www.stayteen.org

Gives honest advice about sex and relationships, including helping teens wait for sex, or providing information about birth control.

Youth Guardian Services
www.youth-guard.org

A Web site run by teens and young adults offering information for gay, lesbian, bisexual, transgendered, straight, and questioning youth.

In Canada
Kids Help Phone
1-800-668-6868

www.kidshelpphone.ca

The 24-hour hotline allows teens to get counseling without giving their names. The Web site also has links to counselors, as well as forums where teens offer support and show you that you are not alone.

Teen Health Source
www.teenhealthsource.com

Advice about teenage sexuality and other health issues run by Planned Parenthood Toronto.

Glossary

contraceptive Birth control device

dental dams Thin pieces of rubber placed over the vagina or anus during intercourse, and over the mouth during oral sex

ejaculates When a penis releases sperm

embryo An egg that has been fertilized by sperm

exploits Adventures; notable deeds

fallopian tubes Two tubes inside a woman's body that link the uterus to her ovaries

fertilized When an egg has met and merged with a sperm

fetus An unborn human baby older than eight weeks

genitalia The organs of the reproductive system, especially the external organs

immune system A system of organs, tissues, and cells that help the body fight disease

menstruation The monthly discharge of blood and other matter from the womb

ovaries The two small parts inside a woman's body, found near the uterus, which produce eggs for fertilization

penis The external male sex organ

puberty A stage of a person's life where hormones help a child grow and develop into an adult

pubic Relating to the area at the front of the pelvis

scrotum The external pouch of a male that contains the testes, which produce semen

sperm Male reproductive cell

uterus The organ inside a woman's body, connected to her vagina and her ovaries, where a fertilized egg goes to grow into a fetus

vaccines Drugs made up of weakened viruses, given, usually by an injection, to increase a person's immunity against certain diseases

vagina Part of the female reproductive tract

viruses Tiny organisms that can multiply inside the living cells of another organism

Index